SUPER SMART INFORMATION STRATEGIES

FIND YOUR WAY ONLINE

by Suzy Rabbat

CHERRY LAKE PUBLISHING • ANN ARBOR, MICHIGAN

A NOTE TO PARENTS AND TEACHERS: Please remind your children how to stay safe online before they do the activities in this book.

A NOTE TO KIDS: Always remember your safety comes first!

CHERRY LAKE Publishing

Published in the United States of America
by Cherry Lake Publishing
Ann Arbor, Michigan
www.cherrylakepublishing.com

Content Adviser: Gail Dickinson, PhD,
Associate Professor, Old Dominion University,
Norfolk, Virginia

Book design and illustration: The Design Lab

Photo credits: Cover and page 1, ©iStockphoto.com/Gisele; page 4, ©AVAVA, used under license from Shutterstock, Inc.; page 8, ©iStockphoto.com/jazzyqt; page 15, ©polusvet, used under license from Shutterstock, Inc.; page 16, ©iStockphoto.com/Belknap; page 18, ©iStockphoto.com/ktsimage; page 23, ©iStockphoto.com/kickstand; page 24, ©Rob Marmion, used under license from Shutterstock, Inc.; page 26, ©iStockphoto.com/lisafx; background art, ©iStockphoto.com/bluestocking

Library of Congress Cataloging-in-Publication Data
Rabbat, Suzy.
Super smart information strategies. Find your way online / by Suzy Rabbat.
p. cm.—(Information explorer)
Includes bibliographical references and index.
ISBN-13: 978-1-60279-639-3 (lib. bdg.)
ISBN-13: 978-1-61080-256-7 (pbk.)
1. Internet searching—Juvenile literature. I. Title. II. Title: Find your way online. III. Series.
ZA4230.R33 2010
025.0425—dc22
2009024549

Cherry Lake Publishing would like to acknowledge the work of The Partnership for 21st Century Skills. Please visit *www.21stcenturyskills.org* for more information.

Printed in the United States of America
Corporate Graphics Inc.
July 2011
CLFA09

Table of Contents

CHAPTER ONE

Starting Your Search

Jack and Emma are getting ready to compete in a chess tournament at school. As they practice, they find that they don't agree on one of the rules. Jack suggests looking online to check the rules. Problem solved!

Information comes in many forms. There are several places where you can look to find it. Many people turn to the World Wide Web for their information. The World Wide Web connects us to billions of Web pages.

Do you like to play chess? You can always learn more strategies. An online search is a great idea!

With a click of your mouse, you can access information on the Web 24/7. Words, video, pictures, and other information are at your fingertips!

As long as you have access to a computer with an internet connection, you can access the Web 24 hours a day, 7 days a week.

There are, however, some challenges in using the World Wide Web. Did you know that nobody is in charge of the Web? People who create Web sites can put any information they like on them. Many Web sites contain valuable information written by experts. But some sites contain information that is incorrect. Other sites contain information that is biased. Biased information is someone's opinion rather than fact.

Finding the right information on the Web can take a long time. To save time and get the right information, you need a Web search strategy! A strategy is a plan that helps you reach your goal. Jack and Emma use strategies to outsmart their opponents in chess. You've probably used a strategy to be successful when playing a video game or a board game. Finding good information is a process that may require several strategies. Let's look at some strategies for searching the World Wide Web.

Smart searchers carefully choose the words for their query, the question they will use for their online search. They identify the important words in their research questions. Then they use those words to build a search strategy. We call these words keywords.

Imagine that your class is beginning a new unit in science. You will be studying the systems of the human body. They include the digestive system, respiratory system, circulatory system, muscular system, and skeletal system. What if you aren't familiar with the body systems? You can get ideas for keywords in reference tools such as encyclopedias and dictionaries. These tools give general information about a topic. By starting your search here, you may come across other words that are connected to your topic. Words that are connected to your topic are called related terms. They have something in common with the topic.

Think about this research question: *Why is a healthy heart an important part of the circulatory system?*

Take a close look at the words in the question. Can you find the keywords or phrases in the question? What are the important words you would use to begin your search? You've got it! The keywords are *circulatory system* and *heart*.

As you begin to read about the circulatory system, you will come across words such as *blood* and *blood vessels*. These words are related terms. They are part of the circulatory system. Add them to your list of keywords. Searching for information about the related terms can help you gather additional helpful information about your topic.

TRY THIS!

Here is another research question to think about. **How do the skeletal and muscular systems affect the way an athlete performs?**

Can you find the keywords? Use those keywords to build a query. Start your search using a general reference tool, such as an encyclopedia or dictionary. As you read about your topic, can you also find related terms and synonyms? If you can, you're on your way to sharpening your search skills!

Once you start to gather keywords, you will come up with a lot of good options.

Imagine trying to find food if the store wasn't organized.

Imagine going to the grocery store with a shopping list. You would expect to find the bananas in the produce aisle. You would look for ice cream in the frozen food section. That's because the store is organized. Grouping similar items together makes it easier to find what you need.

Now consider a store where the items are randomly arranged. The cereal is in the freezer next to the pizza. The milk is sitting on the shelf next to the paper towels. How frustrating! It would take a long time to find what you need. The Web can be like shopping in a disorganized store. Because no one is in charge of the Web, no one is in charge of organizing it!

There are billions of Web sites on the World Wide Web. That can make finding the best information a challenging process. Let's take a look at some of the tools that can help us.

One tool that is commonly used is a search engine. Google is a search engine used by many children and adults. Search engines do not organize the World Wide Web. Instead, they make up for disorganization by helping us navigate through it.

Search engines use special computer programs called Web crawlers to find information on the World Wide Web. Web crawlers build lists of Web sites they find as they "crawl" or search the Web. They remember the words on the Web sites and keep track of the Web addresses to show where those words were found. When you type a keyword in the search box, the search engine matches your keyword with the words on its lists. In seconds, the search engine makes a list of the matching Web sites. Each Web site on the list has a link to take you right to the Web site. The links in this list are called hits.

Search engines are amazing, but remember the Web crawlers are matching your keywords. The results of your search are only as good as the keywords in your query. Try out several keywords, related terms, and synonyms. This will increase your chances of finding the information you need.

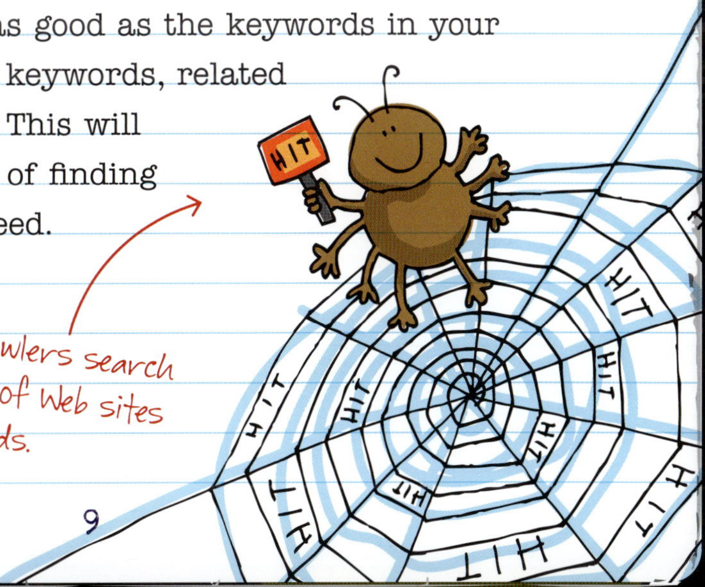

Web crawlers search millions of Web sites in seconds.

TRY THIS!

Your teacher is planning to get a pet for your classroom. Your job is to research possible pets and answer the following question: **Which pet would be the best choice for your classroom?** Here's what to do to begin your search.

1. Structure your query. Look for the keywords in the question. Pet is one keyword. There are many possible animals that make good pets. In this case, however, we can consider only pets that would be suitable for the classroom. The word classroom is another keyword or important word to include in the query.
2. Go to www.google.com and type the two keywords in the search box. Be sure to put one space between each word. Press return to begin your search.

What kind of pet ideas did you come up with when you searched?

Did you Know this?

Google sees all letters as though they were lowercase. It is not important to use capital letters when you type words in the search box—even if one of the words is a proper noun!

Wow! There are more than 2 million hits! Let's look at the results.

Google has a ranking system. Based on your keywords, Google predicts which Web sites will be the most helpful. It puts those sites at the top of your list of hits. Still, some of the Web sites on your list may not be helpful in answering your research question. That's because the ranking is done by computers, not people. For example, some sites will have information about classrooms—classroom furniture, classroom supplies, etc. The Web crawlers are matching the word *classroom* to all the Web sites it can find that contain the word *classroom*. Look through your list of hits. Can you find three sites in your search results that don't look useful?

Or this?

If you spend 1 minute looking at each of the Web sites on your list of results, it will take more than 3 years to look all 2 million Web sites!

Notice that some of the words in your list of hits are underlined in blue. These words are called hyperlinks. Clicking on a hyperlink will take you right to the Web page. Some hyperlinks link you to a different place within the same Web site. Hyperlinks make it quick and easy to get from one place on the Web to another. If you get lost, you can always go back to where you started by clicking on the back arrow in your browser.

Below each hyperlink you'll see a snippet of text. A snippet is a little part. When you use Google, the snippet shows a part of a Web site's text that has the most to do with your search. Other search tools display summaries of the Web sites in their snippets. The snippets will help you determine which hits may supply the best information. Read the snippets in your list of search results. Which three sites look like they would provide the best information about classroom pets?

This is a hyperlink. Hyperlinks are usually blue and underlined.

Choosing a **Classroom Pet**

Classroom Pets can be a HUGE responsibility, so deciding what kind of pet to bring into your classroom is an important decision.

This is the snippet that goes with this hyperlink.

CHAPTER TWO

Narrowing Your Search

You recently discovered that several students in your class are allergic to animals with fur or feathers. That rules out hamsters, gerbils, rabbits, birds, and any other animal covered with fur or feathers. But what about reptiles? They are covered with scales!

This Venn diagram is used to compare two different groups, classroom pets and reptiles. The circle on the left lists common classroom pets. The circle on the right lists some reptiles. The place in the middle, where the circles overlap, shows reptiles that would be suitable classroom pets.

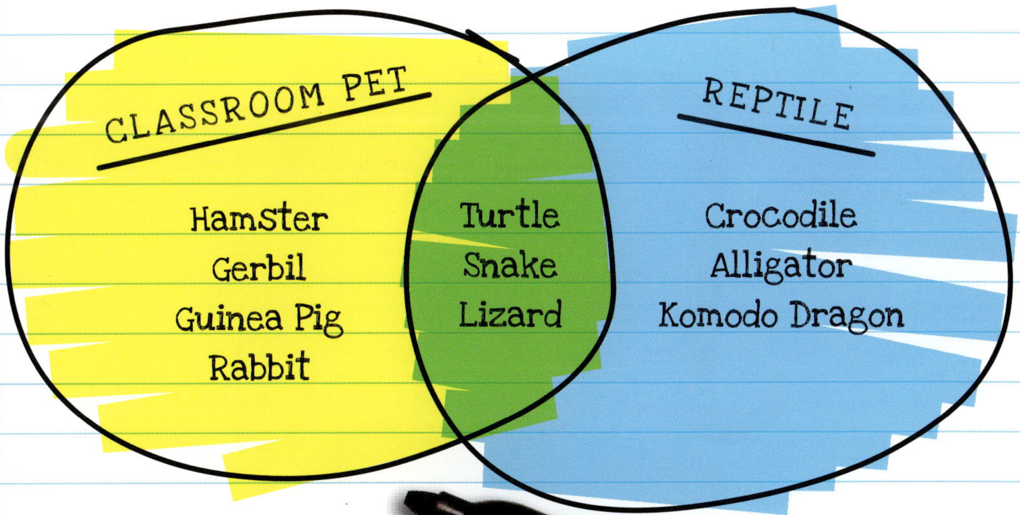

You've already conducted a search for classroom pets. Google's Web crawlers found more than 2 million Web sites to match that query. By adding the keyword *reptiles* to your query, you can narrow your search. When you narrow your search, you are giving the search engine more information about what you need. As a result, you should get fewer hits. These are the items in the space where the circles overlap on the Venn diagram. Adding quotation marks around the words "*classroom pet*" tells the search engine to match those words in that order. This should eliminate unwanted hits for classroom furniture and classroom supplies. Your query would look like this: "classroom pet" reptiles. The search engine will look for information only about classroom pets that are reptiles. Try it and compare the results!

Did narrowing your search help find only reptiles that would make good classroom pets?

TRY THIS!

Structure a new query. Can you think of other keywords you can combine with "**classroom pet**" to narrow down the results? What other living things would make good classroom pets but do not have fur or feathers? Enter your keywords in the search box and see what results you'll find.

Do you think fish make good classroom pets?

Chapter Three: Drilling Down

CHAPTER THREE

Subject Directories Part 1 Drilling Down

You don't need power tools to drill down in a subject directory!

Another helpful tool for finding information on the Web is a subject directory. Subject directories are organized by people, not by Web crawlers. As a result, the sites that are added to the subject directory may contain more reliable information than some of the results you would get from a search engine. Web sites in a subject directory are organized by topic. The topics begin with broad, big ideas. When you click on a topic, you find links to subtopics that fall under that topic. Each time you click on a subtopic, you narrow your search results. This strategy is called the "drill down" strategy. Let's see how it works.

A subject directory usually has a main menu of categories. Pick the category that best describes what you are searching for.

TRY THIS!

KidSpace at the Internet Public Library is a good place to begin. Go to www.ipl.org/div/Kidspace. Take a look at the topics to understand how the information is organized. Notice that some subtopics are listed under each main topic. Where would you begin to search for classroom pets? Under the heading of **Math & Science** there is a subheading for **Animals**. Since a pet is an animal, let's start there. Click on the link for Animals. As you skim the list of subheadings, you'll find a link for Pets. Once you click on Pets, you'll find several links to Web sites about pets. But, how are they organized? Scroll down and see if you can identify a pattern.

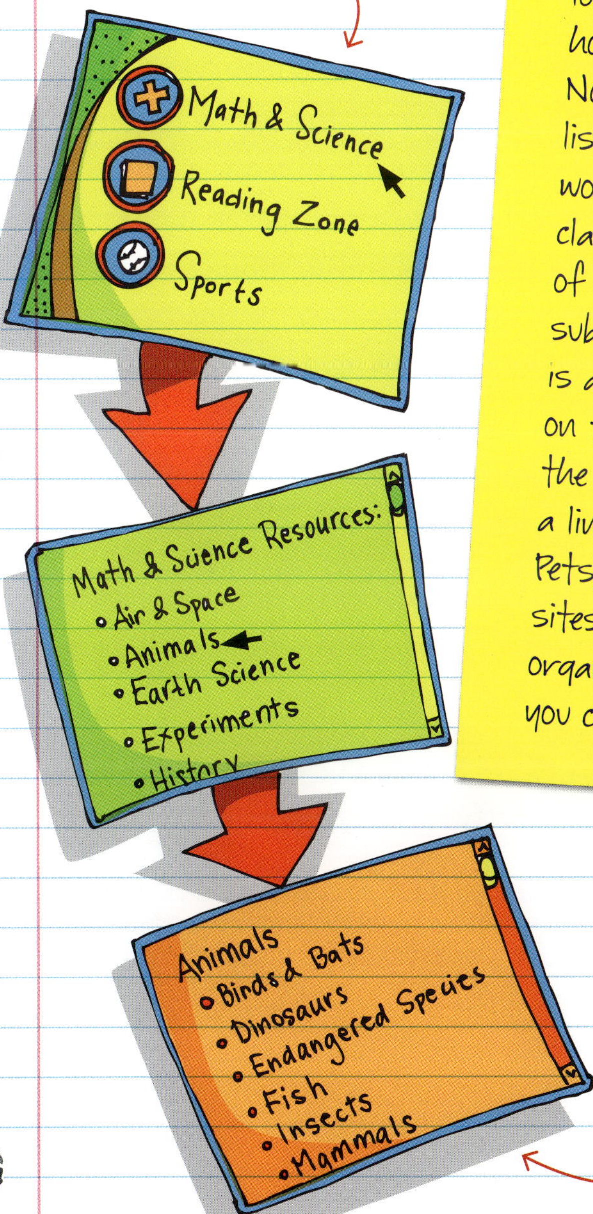

As you drilled down through the screens, did you find ideas for classroom pets?

Did you discover that the hits are listed in alphabetical order by the title of the Web site? Skim the titles to decide which Web site will give you the best information. Don't forget to read the snippets to help you decide which sites to visit first.

Drilling down is a little like traveling through a maze. When you're working your way through a maze, you may come to a dead end. Your only option is to back up and try another path. The same can be said about clicking through the headings and subheadings in a subject directory. If you find your search is not taking you in the right direction, go back to the home page and start on a new path. Drilling down may also give you ideas of related topics to explore.

Getting back to the home page and taking a new path is easier than getting back to the beginning of a maze. It just takes a couple of clicks with your mouse!

TRY THIS!

In addition to finding the perfect classroom pet, you'll need to know how to care for it. Will you need a cage, an aquarium tank, or some other kind of container? What kind of food and climate will your pet need to stay healthy? Use the drill down strategy to learn more about caring for your classroom pet.

What kind of habitat will your new pet need? What type of food does it eat?

CHAPTER FOUR

Subject Directories Part 2 Using Keywords

Many subject directories also have a search field that will allow you to search by keyword. When you enter your keyword, the subject directory looks for Web sites that contain that word. Unlike a search engine, the subject directory does not search the entire World Wide Web. It will match your query only to Web sites that are found in the subject directory.

TRY THIS!

See if you can find some helpful information using a subject directory such as the Internet Public Library, KidsClick, or KidsKonnect. Use the drill down strategy or type your keywords into the search field.

Here's the information problem. Have you ever been curious about space travel? Suppose you wanted to travel to another planet. **What kind of clothing and equipment would you need to survive in space?**

1. Can you identify the keywords in the question above? What other words come to mind when you think about space travel? **Space shuttle**, **astronaut**, **spacecraft**, and **space exploration** are some related terms that would help you locate information about traveling in outer space.

(continued on page 22)

TRY THIS! (CONTINUED)

2. Look at the broad topics on the home page of your subject directory. Where would you most likely find information connected to your keywords?
3. Search by keyword or drill down. Give it a try!

Did you Know this?

Did you know that Pluto is no longer considered a planet? In 2006, scientists created a new definition of **planet**, and Pluto does not fit the definition.

Scientists are discovering new things every day. When you're researching some topics, such as science, it's important to have up-to-date information. Check out the bottom of a Web site's homepage to see when the site was posted or updated.

CHAPTER FIVE

Using a Subscription Database

A third tool for searching the World Wide Web is a **subscription database**. A subscription database is a collection of journal articles, newspapers, documents, or reference books. These materials are only available to those who pay a subscription fee. They are written by people who are experts in their field. Many libraries pay for the subscription that allows its **patrons** to use the database. This means that you have to connect to the database through the library.

Subscription databases require a fee. Your local library is great place to search these databases for free.

Librarians help students of all ages find information online.

A subscription database doesn't retrieve information found in Web sites on the World Wide Web. It searches only for information from the resources that make up that database. Let's say you are looking for information about global warming and climate change. You may find a helpful article in a science journal or in an online encyclopedia that is part of the subscription database.

To search a subscription database, you need log-in information including a user name and password. Ask your public or school librarian about the subscription databases available to you. Find out how you can get a user name and password to search the subscription databases.

You can find specialized databases for these subjects: science, social studies, geography, history, cultures, current events, and literature. Some subscription databases are even designed especially for kids.

Did you Know this?

The information you find online is the intellectual property of the author. That means the ideas, images, and writing belong to the author. When you use someone's ideas in your projects, be sure to show where you found your information by citing your source.

INCLUDE THIS BASIC INFORMATION IN YOUR CITATION:

- AUTHOR'S NAME: Samantha Harvey
- TITLE OF WEB SITE: Solar System Exploration
- DATE IT WAS POSTED OR UPDATED: June 13, 2008
- SPONSORING ORGANIZATION: NASA
- DATE YOU VIEWED IT: May 26, 2009
- THE WEB ADDRESS OR URL: http://... *

A CITATION LOOKS LIKE THIS:

Harvey, Samantha. Solar System Exploration. 13 June 2008. NASA. 26 May 2009 <http://solarsystem.nasa.gov>.

* Some Web addresses can be very long, so just record the information up to the first forward slash. This will help you go back to the source if you want to check your facts. It will also show the reader where you found your information.

Be a responsible user of information. Remember to cite your sources!

TRY THIS!

Check out the Web site for your school or public library. Many public libraries post their subscription databases for kids under the heading **Homework Help**. Once you have your log-in information, choose a database to explore. Does the database specialize in one broad area such as science or does it cover many topics like an encyclopedia does? How do the menu buttons help you navigate through the database?

continued →

If you are having trouble locating or logging into your school's web site, ask your teacher or librarian for help.

Chapter Five: Using a Subscription Database

TRY THIS! (CONTINUED)

As you browse through a database, you may come across interesting topics to explore. Maybe your curiosity will spark some questions to investigate. No questions of your own? Try one of these:

1. Where would you find the world's tallest building?
2. How long does it take for styrofoam to decompose?
3. What animals are currently on the endangered animals list?

How many skyscrapers are there in the world? Try searching online to find the answer!

Subscription databases are a great place to look for authoritative information. If something is authoritative, you can trust the information to be accurate. Although subject directories and subscription databases provide fewer results than a search engine, the results may be a better match for your information need.

No matter where you look for information, it is important to think carefully and evaluate all the information you use. You can do this by checking the information in several sources and comparing the results. You can also check to see if the author has experience or is an expert on the topic. If having the most up-to-date information is important to your topic, check the publication date. Finally, make sure you can read and understand the information you select.

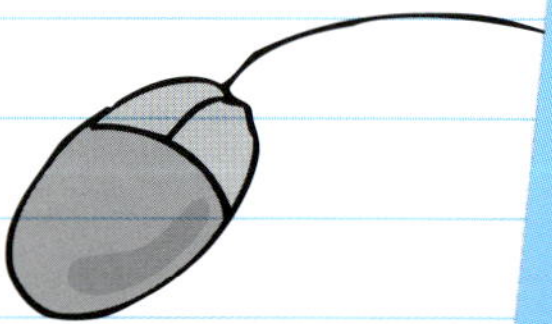

Okay, Smart Searchers! You've practiced some helpful search strategies. You know how to structure a query and narrow your results. You can navigate your way through a search engine, subject directory, or subscription database. You are on your way to becoming smart users of information using online resources!

Smart Search ReSearch Checklist

Think about these questions as you work through the research process.

1. What questions do I have about my topic?
2. What general reference tools can I use to get some big ideas about my topic?
3. What keywords and related terms can I use to structure my query?
4. Which online tools will I use: a search engine, subject directory, or database?
5. Have I shared my ideas with my classmates, teachers, or librarians to get their input on my research?
6. Do I have enough information to solve my information problem? If not, where will I look next?

Glossary

hits **(HITS)** Web sites that are displayed as the result of a search

hyperlinks **(HYE-pur-links)** words that are connected from one Web page to another

intellectual property **(in-tuh-LEK-choo-uhl PROP-ur-tee)** the ownership of ideas, writing, and other creative materials by the person who developed them

keywords **(KEE-wurdz)** important words

patrons **(PAY-truhnz)** customers, people who use a service

post **(POST)** to publish or display information on the World Wide Web

query **(KWIHR-ee)** a question

related terms **(ri-LAY-tid TURMZ)** words that are connected to the topic

search engine **(SURCH EN-juhn)** a tool used to find information on the World Wide Web

subject directory **(SUHB-jikt duh-REK-tuh-ree)** a list of Web resources that is arranged by topic

subscription database **(suhb-SKRIP-shun DAY-tuh-bayss)** a collection of journal articles, newspapers, documents, and reference books that charges a fee for use

Web crawlers **(WEB KRAWL-urz)** computer programs used by search engines to find information

Find Out More

BOOKS

Hamilton, John. *Internet.* Edina, MN: ABDO, 2005.

Oxlade, Chris. *My First Internet Guide.* Chicago, IL: Heinemann Library, 2007.

WEB SITES

Boolify

www.boolify.org/

Learn how to narrow your search with this interactive Web site.

Google SafeSearch

www.squirrelnet.com/search/Google_SafeSearch.asp

Google Safe Search for Kids is a project of educator and search engine expert Mike Reynolds.

KidsClick!

www.kidsclick.org/wows/

This online tutorial for searching the World Wide Web is a project of the Ramapo Catskill Library System.

Index

About the Author

Suzy Rabbat is a National Board certified school librarian. She has two children, Mike and Annie. She lives in Mt. Prospect, Illinois, with her husband, Basile.